To Olivia Rose Paris

Enjoy your book!

Copyright © 2021 Sheila Lebrun-James.

All rights reserved. No part of this book may be used or reproduced by any means, graphic, electronic, or mechanical, including photocopying, recording, taping or by any information storage retrieval system without the written permission of the author except in the case of brief quotations embodied in critical articles and reviews.

Balboa Press books may be ordered through booksellers or by contacting:

Balboa Press
A Division of Hay House
1663 Liberty Drive
Bloomington, IN 47403
www.balboapress.com
844-682-1282

Because of the dynamic nature of the Internet, any web addresses or links contained in this book may have changed since publication and may no longer be valid. The views expressed in this work are solely those of the author and do not necessarily reflect the views of the publisher, and the publisher hereby disclaims any responsibility for them.

Any people depicted in stock imagery provided by Getty Images are models,
and such images are being used for illustrative purposes only.
Certain stock imagery © Getty Images.

Interior Image Credit: Brian Webb

ISBN: 978-1-9822-7822-9 (sc)
ISBN: 978-1-9822-7821-2 (e)

Print information available on the last page.

Balboa Press rev. date: 12/10/2021

This book is dedicated to my heartbeats... Isabella, Chase, and Cameron.

Mommy and Daddy will love you always... even when you don't want to eat.

Mommy and Daddy will love you always... even when you don't listen to them.

Mommy and Daddy will love you always... even when you're not so gentle with your little brother.

Mommy and Daddy will love you always... even when you're using not-so-quiet feet.

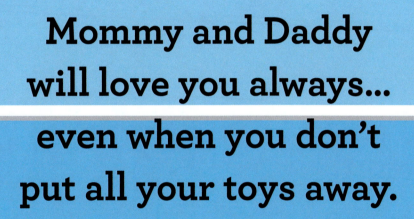

Mommy and Daddy
will love you always...
even when you don't
put all your toys away.

Mommy and Daddy will love you always... even when you find it hard to use your words.

Mommy and Daddy will love you always... even when you don't want to go to bed.

Mommy and Daddy will love you always ...even when you wake us up in the middle of the night.

Mommy and Daddy will love you always because you are and always will be the best thing that has ever happened to us!

Printed in the United States
by Baker & Taylor Publisher Services